Contemplation:
A Year in the Garden

Elin Johnson

Published by Vision Run Publishing
305 Porsmouth Rd., Knoxville, TN 37909
www.VisionRun.com

Photography: Elin Johnson

Printed in the United States

Remembering Charlotte

CONTEMPLATION

Some gardeners can't sit still. They have to concentrate on perfection. Every leaf must be in its place, and they are obsessed with perfection. They cannot relax, but must be busy every minute. Not me!

Every one of my gardens have featured benches prominently, and I've made good use of them. My policy—stop, look, and listen. Enjoy the natural world. Revel in the colors of the flowers and experience the garden's inhabitants— the activity of the birds, a colorful butterfly, or the bees and wasps examining the blossoms. You might even see a bunny or a squirrel. Listen to the wind in the trees and the serenade of the bird calls, and watch the movement of the clouds in the sky. Be still and let the wonder of nature calm you and wash away the stresses of the day.

Sit down awhile and let me share with you some of my memories.

WHO I AM

I am a daffodil in a field of gold.
One blossom among hundreds —
Visible but invisible. Do you know who I am?

I am a feather, carried on the wind —
A memory of things past, never to be again.
Remember when, and when, and when?

I am a grain of beach sand.
Immovable, unable to move;
Then stirred, rearranged helplessly by the tide.

I am a spider, clinging to my web.
Supported perilously by a tiny thread.
I am afraid — suspended in the unknown.

I am an ant carrying a crumb.
Part of a procession following a line:
Predetermined, necessary.

I am my imagination, my hopes for things to come.
Beautiful vistas, heroic deeds, impossibilities —
Meaningful words; but they won't change the world.

I am a kitten, a warm furry ball curled on my cushion.
Alas, the day is late, but I am content.
I am what I have been. It is enough! God is here.

ଡ଼

CAPRICIOUS MARCH

Morning light slanting from the east illuminates everything with a golden glow. From my window I can see points of light sparkling on leaves and branches. It's cold this morning—winter's grasp doesn't want to let go.

Icy frost makes twinkling stars on evergreen leaves and bare branches. The car in the driveway is covered with a white blanket of ice this morning. The cats are reluctant to go outdoors. Little Sister tries to get a drink but the water in the birdbath is frozen solid. I see a squirrel quickly ascend into my neighbor's tree, his fluffy tail outlined in the sunlight.

There are tiny ice sparkles on the green leaves in a pot of pansies beneath the window. Their faces of intense blue-purple smile up at me. Nearby golden daffodils stand tall, oblivious to the cold, and in the front yard yellow violas display cheerful bright clumps. Overhead the bare branches of the red maple are spouting buds of ruby red like beads strung on a silver necklace.

The birds keep still in the branches, seeming to wait for the sun to warm. Warmth will return this afternoon. The cats will lie in the sun and the birds will sing.

March is the month for change. One warm day it seems that spring is here, and the next morning frost will reappear. But be reassured that spring really is near. In the meantime I will enjoy the miracle of each tiny spring flower in the certainty that each week is another step in the progression of the wonder of nature.

CS

AND THE MOCKINGBIRD WATCHES

At the front door I hesitate—
A gray bird swings on a twig of the tree just outside the door:
A dogwood—adorned with the last of the red berries, a treat for birds.
The twig bounces up and down; he gobbles berries eagerly.
He flies to the redbud, and I emerge to retrieve the mail;
      And the Mockingbird watches.

I sit alone on the concrete bench on a warm February day—
Two male cardinals flash by, brilliant scarlet against the blue sky.
Each competes for the right to bring his mate to this yard.
One wins the short confrontation and flies toward the red hollies:
Sparkleberries at the edge of the road—a victory reward.
      And the Mockingbird chases him away.

In the blue spruce outside my window—
The gray bird sits surveying the yard. I see his dark eye stripe.
He looks intently at something. It is the orange cat walking by.
Where will the cat go? Will he be interested in catching birds?
Or is he just moving toward a sunny place for a nice nap?
      The Mockingbird watches, carefully.

I hear a sound—a sound I hate. It is a chain saw, the enemy of the trees.
It is not far away. The city road crew is mutilating trees today.
I shudder; then notice a gray presence in the maple tree.
Could he possibly understand the significance of the sound?
Is it my imagination that he looks uneasy?
      But the Mockingbird just watches quietly.

Yesterday it was warm enough to work outdoors—
I raked the lower garden and then pulled weeds. There are so many!
Wild strawberries—their runners meander everywhere.
And the wild mustard must be pulled before they broadcast their seeds.
But this was not a chore; it was exhilarating to escape the house.

     And the Mockingbird watched me.

Then today a grand ritual of spring begins—
The mockingbird has a companion. They strut back and forth
Rather like a fencing match: one advancing and the other retreating,
Then they reverse the order of their dance. Spring is coming!
They will build their nest and make a family. Continuity is eternal!

     And the Mockingbird will keep watch!

☙

MEMORIES

What treasure do I find today?
What treasure have I found?
Tiny bluets; like years ago
while lying on the ground.

Beautiful to a lonely child--
their tiny faces smiled at me.
With violets blue, leaves like fans,
and yellow jonquils growing free.

Moss like soft green carpet
formed my playhouse floor.
Acorn cups my dishes,
rocks outlined the door.

I looked at clouds in sky of blue
through cherry blossoms white.
Leaned back against the dark red trunk
and everything seemed right.

Bees danced upon the dandelions
that bloomed nearby the tree.
And high among the blossoms
they buzzed spring harmony.

I see these things today
as if no time had passed.
I'll see them always in my mind
until the very last.

ℭ

MY FANTASY

Every winter I spend a good deal of time browsing the flower
catalogs and making plans for my garden for the following
summer. Somewhere in my contemplations I remembered an
even better escape from reality. In the old series, *Star Trek: The Next Generation* the
Starship Enterprise had a holodeck, a place where a supercomputer would conjure
up your fantasies holographically and make them appear in real time. You could
even share your heroic adventures with friends. What a wonderful concept!

Computer: Create a flawless garden ringed by dark green conifers except
for openings here and there—one framing a view of horses grazing in an open
field and one with a magnificent view of the mountains. The soil will be of such
perfect consistency that a trowel can be inserted effortlessly. The grass will never
need to be mowed. There will be a sunny area filled consecutively with spring

bulbs, then iris, roses, Asiatic lilies, daylilies, and late summer flowers. In the spring, there will be no out-of-season hot days to melt the azalea blossoms. Slugs to attack the hostas will be unknown, and there will never be long hot, dry spells in the summer to stunt them. Rains will fall regularly, very gently, and only at night. The days will always be sunny (except for an occasionally billowy white cloud) and the temperature will always be somewhere between 75 and 85 degrees with low humidity. Roses will not be plagued with black spot. They will bloom continuously all summer, and there will be no Japanese beetles. I will have no problem growing blue hostas, delphiniums, or Mediterranean type plants. My cats and dog will be very well behaved and never bark or jump in someone's lap. People will come from miles around to marvel at my exceptional garden, and I will be a beautiful, gracious hostess dressed for a tea party that I will conduct in the shade garden (there won't be any flies, either).

Does this sound like the kind of daydream one might have while perusing the plant catalogs? Unfortunately, there comes a time when the bubble bursts and we are faced with reality. If you drop by in April you will find me pulling weeds in my jeans and old T-shirt, trying to catch up. I might have some pretty spots in my yard, but there will also be eyesores. And I will be completely helpless to avoid whatever type of weather there might happen to be.

Nevertheless, I always enjoy every minute of every pretty day in the spring, and will go on to revel in the progression of flowers all summer despite whatever hardships I may face.

છ

TINY TREASURES

Last year's fallen leaves left a carpet of brown.
Early spring is the time to look all around.
To find tiny treasures—blue, yellow and pink.
Well worth a search for their blossoms, I think!

First are the crocus—precursors of spring.
Each little brown corm will eventually bring
A bright puddle of color, a welcoming sight—
First golden yellows, then purples, then whites.

Daffodils are showy—big bang for the bucks.
But little ones peep through like wee baby ducks.
Gold flowers so cheerful, wet from the rain
Sparkle so brightly in sunlight again.

Lovely pink tulips (their name I have lost)
Peep through the junipers creeping across.
Much like their Turkish mountainside source
Their dry sunny bank a good home, of course.

Observe the grape hyacinths, tiny blue bells
Carpet the ground with Wedgewood blue cells.
Their seeds are prolific — over the years
They'll fill up the spaces, the sweet little dears.

Look for these treasures when cold tries to stay.
They really last longer when heat stays away.
You'll never find them when summer is here.
They'll sleep underground; next spring reappear.

I have always looked for treasures every time I enter my garden in the spring. Every year I look for reemergence of my familiar friends—the bulbs. Every day will reveal a few more of my treasures. This is a ritual I enjoy every spring.

I like to have a group of daffodils here, another group over there, and scattered plantings of tulips and crocus up and down the path instead of having a large display of one kind in one place. The big displays are gorgeous for a short period, but then they are gone. And if there should be a late freeze or wind storm, they could be destroyed. If you have a succession of bulbs and spring blooming shrubs and trees you can have something beautiful in bloom every day for a long time.

Happy Spring!

CB

JOIN THE PARTY

You're invited to a party—
Festivities in full swing.
The plants have started blooming,
The birds are on the wing.

Jonquils act like Cinderella,
Pansies dance upon the wall.
Tulips in bright red dresses
Have themselves a ball!

The redbud in its Easter dress

Is lavender perfection.

Crabapple ruffles pink and white

Bob in all directions.

Bees sip from apple blossoms

Drawn by their perfume.

Viburnum's fragrant punch cups

Spice up the garden room.

Join the party, everyone!

Just put aside your duty.

Gaze upon our wondrous world

And revel in its beauty!

ভ

CONTEMPLATION

My relief is indescribable when golden daffodils bloom.

Spring's return renews my spirits.

Winter is behind—the progression has begun!

I listen with excitement when a flock of geese flies near.

Their voices reflect happy anticipation—

surging together toward their destination!

I search April's garden for wildflowers waking from their rest.

Ephemeral beauties! They come silently

but then are gone, to delight again another time.

I feel the timelessness of moss covered mountain rocks.

How long they have watched our passing...

How insignificant we really are.

I savor the odor of damp soil when a summer rain begins:

an elemental experience

as basic as life itself.

21

My soul is uplifted when bright flowers bloom in June.

An explosion of color fills my eyes—

an eagerly awaited procession of brilliance.

I contemplate diversity in the buzz of myriad insects in July.

All seek the flower's pollen: nature's bounty.

Each is unique, but all have common goals.

I reflect on the fragility of delicate butterfly wings.

Most wondrous of creatures!

Brilliantly hued miracles floating in the air.

I enjoy the companionship of orange kitties purring at my feet.

Their love for me is constant—

unaffected by insignificant slights.

My face is cooled by the wind when a thunderstorm approaches.

The sky boils with dark clouds.

Exhilaration builds in my consciousness.

I am filled with wonder when the leaves of autumn blaze.

The world is a cathedral lit by golden autumn light

far surpassing any human endeavor.

My mind is thoughtful when I study a stately winter tree at sunset.

Starkly beautiful, its buds are next year's promise —

its silhouette dark against the rosy sky.

My heart swells with gratitude to God for my garden and its inhabitants!

It is my sanctuary for peaceful contemplation —

reassuringly dependable but forever new.

CB

HIGH SUMMER

I t's July 5— high summer. Everything is at the peak of bloom— daylilies, lilies, heleniums and purple coneflowers. The knock-out roses have started their second bloom. Coleus, geraniums and zinnias are in bloom in my pots set off by blue angelonias and green foliage plants.

I sit on the deck and enjoy the panorama of summer. The sky is blue, and there are white thunderclouds in the east toward the mountains. The cats have arranged themselves in several locations— lazy in the summer heat. They try to ignore the occasional fire cracker that goes off in the neighborhood, saved by little boys from the cacophony of the night before.

The garden is alive with insects— butterflies, bumblebees and wasps— all reveling in the bounty of mid-summer. Happiness may be "a warm puppy," but it is also a bumblebee gathering pollen from a purple coneflower. They seem to wiggle with delight while crawling about on the yellow stamens. You can see fat yellow pantaloons on their back legs—pollen to be flown back to their nest.

Butterflies love the zinnias and lantanas best, along with tall purple verbena

bonariensis. An inventory of one clump of purple coneflower today included six small brown or tan skipper butterflies, a yellow sulphur, and two orange butterflies, as well as half a dozen fat bumblebees. Several white cabbage butterflies fluttered above them, playing tag on the terrace.

Oh! Look up into my neighbor's wild cherry tree. The cherries are ripe, and the whole bird community is taking part in the feast— robins, cardinals, grackles, and a procession of small birds. The blue jay yells "thief" at the others (although he doesn't mean it— there's plenty for all), and there is even a woodpecker drumming on a limb. The birds are like high flying acrobats in a circus, hanging upside down to reach the fattest, most choice cherries. They are also enjoying the sprinkler running in the backyard.

In the top of the cherry tree the mockingbird overlooks it all and sings a loud, glorious song— a veritable celebration of summer. Maybe I should join him. I, too, feel like celebrating the magnificence of nature in this most exciting of seasons. (I know, of course, I'd look ridiculous— but maybe I don't care). A house wren flies to the dogwood and begins fussing loudly; but he changes to a song when he is joined by his family, and they fly from tree to tree.

Consider the wrens

My noisy good friends

Searching for bugs in the garden.

And see how the bees

Examine the trees

And flowers—for bright yellow pollen.

Watch butterflies flit

Then sip a bit

Of nectar in every bright blossom.

And I just observe

As they hover and swerve—

A panoply of nature happening!

ଊ

A RAINY AFTERNOON IN JUNE

One morning in June there was a rain shower. It didn't last long, and after it was over I went out to fill the bird feeders. Most of the time a heavy rain will cause daylily flowers to dissolve or wilt, but this light shower just placed raindrops on their petals. They were very pretty. The yellow one with the red throat is Don Stevens, and it's my very favorite (today).

Daylilies are pretty,

whether smooth edged or frilly.

Each one's a beauty,

a show-stopper, really!

There's a color to match up

with each Millie or Tilly.

And a clump can be placed here

and there wvilly-nilly!

I look for them in summer

in both flat yards or hilly.

My favorite? All of them,

each one's a dilly!

(Isn't this verse silly?)

CB

THE MOCKINGBIRD NEST

There was a round raised bed outside my breakfast room window in my yard in Sweetwater. I had planted numerous daffodils in the bed to bloom in the spring and then daylilies and tall lilies in summer.

One day around the first of July, 2016, two of my friends came to visit. One of them was looking at the hibiscus standard in the middle of the round bed, and she said, "There's a bird nest." I looked where she was pointing and, sure enough, there was a nest. I went over and looked and there were eggs inside. I watched it in the coming days and discovered it was a mockingbird nest. Mockingbirds have lived in my yard ever since I moved here, but I had not noticed that nest.

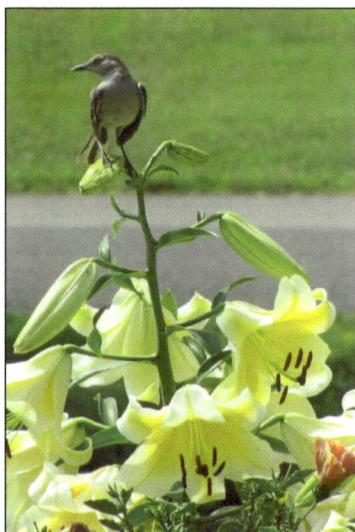

This was not the best place for a nest, and I was pessimistic about the success of these birds. On July 4, my family gathered at my house. I showed them the nest, and some of them made pictures. At that time the birds had just hatched, and you could see the little beaks open, waiting for food (for some reason, I didn't make a picture myself). I was still not optimistic these babies would be able to mature— it was terribly hot, and at that time it was also awfully dry. I was afraid to turn on the sprinkler, but finally decided that if I didn't the hibiscus was going to die. A few days later I checked on them, and the little birds were growing fast.

Fast forward two or three weeks. I had checked on several occasions and confirmed that the baby birds were indeed still alive. Then one morning from the breakfast room I noticed activity at the nest. I grabbed my camera and watched to find out what was going on. The babies were ready to leave the nest. By the time I got ready to make pictures the last little bird was standing on the side of the nest trying to gain enough courage to leave.

After a while it jumped out onto the ground below, and then I watched from the window as there was movement in the foliage. Finally the little bird came over to the wall of the raised bed, and the mother bird convinced it to flutter in short hops over to the relative safety of the holly bushes next to the house.

I think the babies stayed in the holly bushes for several days. Hollies are dense bushes, and I never got close enough to photograph them, but the parent birds continued to fly in with food. Finally, sometime after the first of August I watched two birds out my window. They were about the same size, but one of them was obviously still begging for food. It would fluff its wings and open its beak, but the mother would just fly away. I guess she had decided the young bird was old enough to hunt its own food. It was such fun to watch this drama from my window. Hooray! The nest was successful!

ೞ

LATE SUMMER

My, oh my, it's awful hot!
No one can deny it's not.
Two more months seems like a lot.
But then the heat will be forgot.

At least I do not need to mow —
Dead grass will no longer grow.
Remember when hot days go slow:
Seasons come and seasons go.

The summer sun is merciless! It was 95 degrees today, and it hasn't rained in several days. The sun is moving toward the horizon now, and the air is cooling; but when I look around I find evidence of the sun's relentless assault. Although I watered the lower garden yesterday, the plants in the containers down there are already wilting and they have to be to be watered this evening without fail if they are to remain beautiful. In this heat one day can be the difference between beauty and devastation. How do the trees survive? How do the native plants in the woodlands live through such extremes of heat and drought?

The sun is low in the sky, and its rays backlight plants in my line of sight. The hardy begonias which appear plain green when the sun is overhead now show bright red veining where the sun's rays angle into their clump. There are three clumps of ferns in line from where I sit to the west, and I see the outline of their beautiful fronds turned golden in the sun's rays—a tracery of green-gold lace. Surely their foliage is the most beautiful of all the plants.

I hear the water dropping in another part of the garden where the sprinkler is running. The birds know it is there and come to take advantage of the temporary relief from the hot, dry day. They enjoy it so much I almost feel obligated to run the sprinkler for them every day.

It's incredible how many insects and birds frequent my garden. It's almost like a flowery island in the middle of a desert. The drier the surrounding yards become the more bees and wasps come to my well-watered yard. They almost fight over the flower heads. And I have more hummingbirds than usual. I'm sure other gardeners who water their gardens have the same experience.

Deadheading is a never-ending job. I spend the morning watering and snapping off the spent daylilies and other blossoms. This morning I started to cut off a pink zinnia because it looked ragged, then stopped to look. There in the middle of the flower was a tiny caterpillar, and like a chameleon it had turned pink, too, so it would be invisible to its predators. Isn't nature wonderful!

There are so many plants in my garden that must be watered if they are to survive. August is still ahead! Can they be protected through the extreme heat, or will I forget one day and inadvertently fail to water? My plants seem almost like children that must be protected. Guess I'll just go on watering.

My, oh my, it's awful hot!
Let me find a shady spot.
Even there it's really not
Cool enough to like a lot.

When my clothes are wringing wet
And I mop my brow from sweat
I wish for autumn. Then we'll get
Cooler days — relief, I'll bet!

☙

A LUCKY DAY

In spite of the drought my garden is aglow with color, thanks primarily to the daylilies. Sitting in the shady spot at the end of the deck looking down on the terrace I see the bees working the purple beebalm below. And looking into a showy clump of daylilies, Holiday Delight, a brilliant red-orange variety with a bright red throat, is like looking into a bonfire. This one makes so many buds that it easily has 20 blooms open at a time.

I have been sitting here reading with my feet propped up on a small table, and every now and then I look up and watch the little white cabbage butterflies attending to the pink carpet of creeping thyme blossoms between the stepping stones. The scent of the golden yellow Anaconda lilies beside the

tool shed reaches me, and the purple coneflowers blooming beside them makes a pretty picture.

Then I am diverted from my reading by a sound. What was that rumble? Could it be thunder in the distance? I look around and, sure enough, there is a cloud moving this way from Loudon County—looks like they may be getting some rain. Will it be a lucky day and reach us here, or will it veer away like it does so often? Is it possible that I won't have to water tonight?

In the next half hour or so I watch the clouds move ever so slowly this way and listen as the thunder grows louder. The cloud is beautiful—gray pillows of air moving, tossing, rearranging—like fondant candy boiling in a pan. I have always loved watching the approach of storm clouds. Anticipating their force is inherently exciting.

The swifts that live in the chimneys over at the grammar school start riding the air currents, having a great time. And I see a buzzard circling high up in the air, but the wind carries him out of sight behind the oak tree. The cardinals that live in the yard fly back and forth as if anticipating that rain is imminent, and a chickadee lights in the service berry tree next to the deck and chatters with excitement. More and more of the swifts join the game and fly around and around over my head. They circle and dive with great enjoyment. The wind has become cooler and more intense.

The cats gather around me, seeming to know that it may be nearing time to go inside. Little Sister sits on the railing enjoying the wind through her fur.

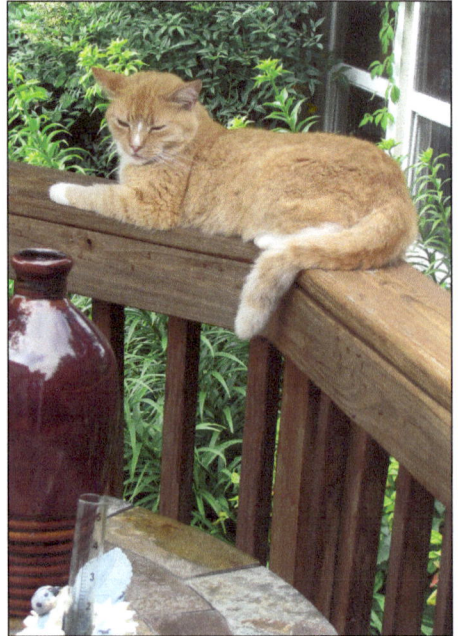

Then it occurs to me that the thunder is receding and the sound is coming from another direction. But the wind is still blowing hard. The temperature has dropped even further, and it's wonderful sitting here on the deck enjoying the cool breeze. Suddenly I become aware of a damp odor—rain—and almost immediately hear the sound of raindrops falling on my neighbor's metal roof. The cats and I scurry for the door with great big drops falling around us. From the porch we watch the rain fall. Beautiful rain!

***

It didn't last long, but the rain was really appreciated. A lucky day? I don't know. I forgot to bring my cordless phone in with me.

CB

LOOK SKYWARD

Lift your eyes upward into the blue.

Look right around you; sample the view.

The palette of autumn appears everywhere.

See the great colors—here, there, and there!

Red, gold and amber glow in the sun—

Here purple, there orange, brilliant each one.

The blue sky behind them enhances the hues.

Magnificent autumn! Masterpiece renewed.

The colors of the trees in our East Tennessee gardens and the countryside around us is really a great gift. Everywhere we look we are surrounded by the colors of autumn. In October the dark reds of the dogwoods, the bright reds of the sourwoods, and yellow leaves of the redbuds appear. Then the maples, the belles of the fall, begin their technicolor picture show of yellow, orange and red. The Japanese maples follow with their brilliant shades that may be the most beautiful of all. In November the golden colors of the poplars and hickories are all around us, and lastly the oaks display their rusty browns.

In my little town of Sweetwater, Tennessee there are many maple trees planted in front yards. Many of them are very old, and you can stand under them and look up through their branches. How spectacular the colors and shapes of the branches! I lived in an older section of town where many displayed their exceptional colors, and I was able to appreciate them every year.

The mountains are nearby, and everyone tried to make an annual trip to enjoy the exceptional view of the colors in the forests there. How fortunate I was to live there!

The autumn leaves are glowing

Like sun thru clear stained glass.

This year's color spectacle

Seems all others to surpass.

My dogwood is a lovely purple red,

The burning bush scarlet fire.

The maples all around me —

Gold and orange to admire.

Yellows clear as lemon Jell-O,
Orange — campfire flame.
Red like parrot feathers,
Purple and red wine the same.

The last of the Knock-out roses

Complete the brilliant view

Providing exclamation points—

Remaining red petals askew.

Ah, window panes need washing;

The laundry must be done.

What will we have for supper?

Spaghetti for everyone?

But still I sit here watching.

As if in a kind of trance.

Seems somehow more important

To watch the leaves' last dance.

So ephemeral! They're so fleeting!

Tomorrow they will fall.

I'll absorb this day's beauty

All winter to recall.

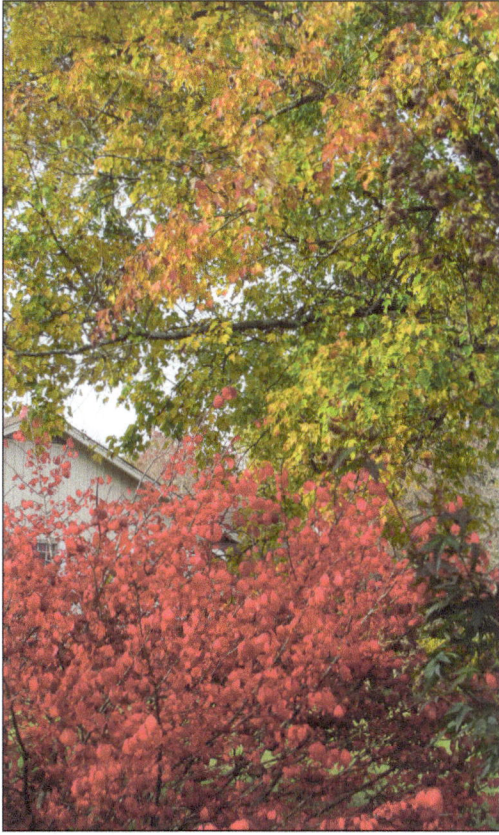

The colors of autumn are so special! Fruits and berries add dots of red and orange to the scene, and the grasses, with their graceful, curving blades, dance in the breeze.

All the colors are emphasized by the blue of the sky which is never as brilliant as in autumn. Then when the sun begins to move low in the sky everything seems to be washed with a golden glow. No wonder it's hard to turn away. Look skyward and soak in the beauty! When the trees are cloaked with coats of gorgeous color, most neighborhoods are beautiful gardens.

Look right around you and sample the view in your own neighborhood. Enjoy!

☙

THE YEAR REMEMBERED

April's jonquils and tulips

Meant end of cold at last.

May's peonies and iris

Brought memories of the past.

June brought lilies red and gold.

July's flowers were myriad hue.

Asters and black-eyed Susans

In August we could view.

And there were roses, pink and white

And lovely butterflies flew about.

Bees were buzzing all around —

Blue salvia was their choice, no doubt.

September was the time for pause,

To contemplate the summer.

The month to add plants here and there,

And toss some that were bummers.

But October was the beginning

Of autumn's super display.

Nature's matchless masterpiece—

Enjoy it every day!

Immerse yourself in the color.

Let it flow over you.

Celebrate this year's beauty.

Always remembered, ever new!

ଔ

WINTER GREEN

Green is the color of winter.
Not gray; no, green is here.
Green is the color of promise —
potential for the upcoming year.

Observe the cedar's dark, dark green
(native Christmas tree).
Sprouting everywhere it seems —
majestic if left to be.

Pyramid of refuge for the birds —
a shield from wind and snow.
Gray berries are a favorite treat
for mockingbirds, you know.

Rhododendron's rounded candles
herald next spring, I think.
Such a miracle — small pointy buds
will produce huge balls of pink.

Hollies are the happiest
of all our winter trees,
adorned with bright red Christmas balls
for all the world to see.

Green is everywhere you look:
box, pine, spruce, and yew.
And a magnificent magnolia
Completes the winter view.

ଓ

EAST TENNESSEE WINTERTIME

One winter day I traveled from Sweetwater to my daughter's home in Sevierville: through the country on Hwy 322 to Vonore and then Hwy. 411 to Maryville and then Seymour and then east to Sevierville. It was a marvelous sunny morning. There was frost on the ground, and the sun that was low in the sky created long shadows across the fields. On the way I began to think about the beauty of our area.

First and foremost is the presence of green. The most prominent green in the countryside is that of the cedars—beautiful pyramids of dark green. They appear in a wide variety of sizes because their berries are distributed so extensively by the birds. In some areas their shapes are narrow, reminiscent of garden cultivars in the catalogs. In others they are fat and fluffy. A mature cedar has a distinctive sculptural gray trunk unlike any other tree. I have always loved the cedars. My father used to take us out into the country every year to find our Christmas tree (with permission from the farmer, of course). The fragrance of a cedar tree will always be a Christmas memory to me. And you never knew what you would find when you brought it in—maybe a bird nest or cocoons. Daddy would hold up his hands to gauge the height; he tried to pick a tree that would almost touch the living room ceiling, and he almost always succeeded.

The year I was twelve mother took me to Knoxville to pick out a new coat (an early Christmas present and a major expenditure in those days). It was a beautiful, green wool coat with big buttons, and I was so proud of it. Obviously I shouldn't have worn it on that day, but when Daddy decided to go hunt a tree that afternoon I grabbed it and my brother and I ran to the car. Daddy led the way across the fields. He was familiar with the farm because he went there from time to time to hunt quail and doves, so he knew where the cedars grew. We had to stop occaisionally and get across a barbed wire fence, usually by crawling underneath. Unfortunately, trying to hurry at one fence I managed to snag my coat on a barb and tore a triangular hole in the back of my coat. We came home with a beautiful cedar tree, but my mother could have killed me! I wore a coat with a darned spot for a long time.

Another significant green in the winter landscape is that of the pines. Pines are varied in the way they grow. To most people who live in this area they are synonymous with groves of pines with tall straight trunks extending into the canopy. There are other types, however. A white pine planted where it has room will grow into a stately pyramid with soft blue-green needles, one of the most beautiful of trees. And everyone is familiar with the loblolly pine farms. In the 1930's this area was a textbook example of poorly managed farms with soil so eroded not much would grow. I can remember how pathetic the hillsides looked with exposed yellow clay gullies. Beginning in the 1950's pine farming became widespread, and we watched them evolve: small pyramids emerging in rows in a fallow field; then a green expanse of medium sized trees with the ground covered with brown pine needles at their feet; then lines of tall straight trunks with brown alligator skin textured bark. And we got used to seeing the log trucks loaded with trunks like huge stacked toothpicks.

But there are other pines, too. My neighbor has mugo pines, small cushions of soft green that are wonderful landscape plants. Japanese black pines and cultivars of Scotch pine also make great garden specimens. But I have a soft spot for the scrub pines that come up in disturbed land where very little else will grow. I saw one during my drive that day back lit by the slanting winter sun. Its trunk was gnarled and crooked and it was covered with cones. Nature has a way of renewing itself even in difficult circumstances. I remember once standing beneath a similar tree and watching a chickadee pecking seeds out of one of the cones.

There are other significant evergreens. The hollies are most reminiscent of the Christmas season with their beautiful red berries. This year they are laden with berries, making up for last year's barren winter after the late freeze. There are not many along the highway, but I would occasionally see one in a yard beside the road. And once in a while a magnificent magnolia can be seen(there are a number of them in Sweetwater). Both the hollies and magnolias are havens for birds, particularly in the late winter. And they are my great winter companions—hollies in my yard and a huge magnolia in my neighbor's.

When my husband was in the Air Force we lived in Indiana for two years. This was a flat world covered in snow all winter, and I missed the green of East Tennessee terribly. But it was not only the greenery, I missed the hills and woodlands of East Tennessee. Highlighted by the slanting sun, the view across an East Tennessee field usually terminates with a woodland or a line of small trees that have grown up in a fence row, good habitat for wildlife.

The shapes of the bare deciduous trees are like sculptures, many of them recognizable by their individual shapes. Nothing is more magnificent than a large oak tree, and they are beautiful in all seasons. There used to be many of them years ago, but now they are a rare treat. These trees are veritable giants, symbols of strength. The silhouette of the hackberry trees is notable for many tiny twigs on the ends of the branches that remind me of lacework. You have to look closely to see the pendulous miniature berries that are so important to all kinds of birds in the winter. And the dogwoods are easily identifiable to East Tennesseans in winter with their tightly folded gray buds waiting for spring when their beautiful white blossoms will unfurl. When the leaves fall, surprises sometimes reveal empty nests where birds raised their families last summer, hidden in the foliage, undiscovered.

I looked for other lifetime friends on this trip—the sycamores— stately white skeletons. As a rule they signify the presence of water, usually one of the numerous creeks in our area. From a country road in East Tennessee, a meandering row of gleaming white trunks is proof that a stream flows there. Weeping willows accompany them, and in early spring the willows will turn chartreuse green long before other leaves appear. I searched for the stark white branches of the sycamores deliberately on this trip, and they became more numerous the closer to Sevierville I got. This surprised me since I equate them with valley scenarios.

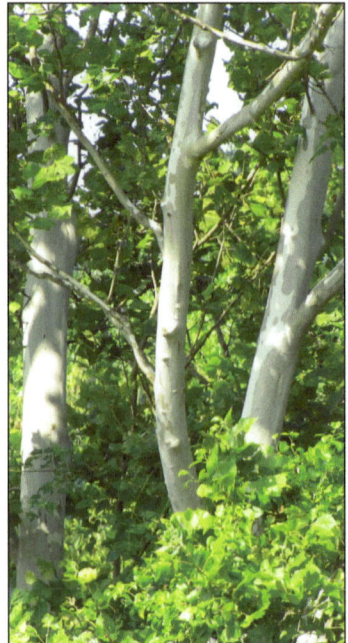

On this day the sun highlighted many wooded areas where red oaks in the edge of the woods retained their leaves, shining like burnished copper in the sunlight. Other trees, the hickories, maples, and many others, were bare, their silhouettes outlined against the blue sky.

Between Maryville and Seymour the mountains were a constant presence beside me—giving me a comforting sense of enclosure. The view across the fields toward the mountains represents a feeling of home. Then in Seymour I turned toward the mountains, and the rest of my journey took me closer to them. At my daughter's home they were visible from her windows—an undulating blue outline nearby.

On the way home the setting sun turned the sky deep pink, and the red sun was reflected in the water as I crossed the bridge over the Little Tennessee (now Tellico Lake). Then the trees on top of the knobs between Madisonville and Sweetwater were silhouetted against the sky, the shapes of the bare trees a beautiful promise of the verdant forest that will return next spring. Winter in East Tennessee is never boring--if you look closely you can always find the promise of beauty to come.

Ↄ

BRING ON THE SNOW!

What a beautiful snow! It measured six inches here, and my little dog, Sparky, leaped around all over this morning. He stopped from time to time to taste the snow then would jump around some more. He didn't stay out as long as usual, though—he must have decided the warm house was a better place to be.

The birds sat in the Japanese maple outside my breakfast room window and waited patiently for me to bring their seeds. At one time there were six doves sitting there in the little tree. Their breasts were puffed up in the cold, and they waited patiently, maybe dreaming of the seeds they hoped I would bring.

I ventured out only once that morning to deliver the seeds and then proceeded out to the mailbox. I walked in the tracks Sparky had made and had no problem except where the snow plow had left piles at the side of the road.

Much of my time in winter is spent looking out my breakfast room windows. One faces south toward the road, and the other is an east window toward the rising sun. These are my windows on the winter world!

I saw from my window that morning
Blue shadows on pristine snow.
Wonders I experienced that day—
Sights not often known.

Networks of dark tree branches
Were outlined against the white—
Lovely black ink tracery—
Masterpieces framed just right.

Shapes were noticeably outlined.
I sat there mesmerized:
Mounds, pyramids, sentinels;
Arching branches—sights highly prized.

The morning light was blinding,
Reflected in the snow.
But now the day nears ending.
Oh, I so enjoyed the show!

෯

(THEY ARE SLEEPING!)

Holidays are special—

Families, food, and fun!

Festive decorations

And traditional things are done.

Flower beds are forgotten.

Heck, it's cold outside.

Savor your Christmas turkey

And admire your tree with pride.

Meanwhile, out in the garden
The flowers are sleeping sound—
Happily dormant underground
While morning frosts abound.

Enjoy the holidays while they're here.
But the time is far away
When the garden will awaken
On a sunny warm spring day.

So during the long, long winter
Ensconced in your easy chair,
Envision next year's garden
And lovely blossoms growing there.

∛

ELIN JOHNSON is a Master Gardener born and raised in East
Tennessee. For 33 years she commuted an hour each way to her job at a
large paper mill leaving her with little free time. She began gardening in
earnest after her retirement, and during the next 20 years developed two
gardens. One of her properties was a small lot on a steep hillside, divided
into "garden rooms". It was mostly shady with mature trees and shrubs.
Then she moved to a larger property with flat and sunny land. She now
lives in a condo with a small garden in Knoxville, TN. She moved there
with her favorite plants, hostas and daylilies.

www.ingramcontent.com/pod-product-compliance
Lightning Source LLC
Chambersburg PA
CBHW040929030426
42334CB00002B/21